CHOOSING SIMPLICITY

CHOOSING SIMPLICITY

EMBRACING THE BENEFITS OF A SIMPLER LIFE

Margaret Feinberg

Foreword by Luci Swindoll

THOMAS NELSON
Since 1798

NASHVILLE   DALLAS   MEXICO CITY   RIO DE JANEIRO

Published in Nashville, Tennessee, by Thomas Nelson. Thomas Nelson is a registered trademark of Thomas Nelson, Inc.

Thomas Nelson, Inc., titles may be purchased in bulk for educational, business, fund-raising, or sales promotional use. For information, please e-mail SpecialMarkets@ThomasNelson.com.

Unless otherwise noted, Scripture quotations are taken from the NEW KING JAMES VERSION. © 1982 by Thomas Nelson, Inc. Used by permission. All rights reserved.

Scripture quotations marked NIV are taken from the HOLY BIBLE: NEW INTERNATIONAL VERSION®. © 1973, 1978, 1984 by International Bible Society. Used by permission of Zondervan Publishing House. All rights reserved.

Scripture quotations marked *The Message* are taken from *The Message* by Eugene H. Peterson. © 1993, 1994, 1995, 1996, 2000. Used by permission of NavPress Publishing Group. All rights reserved.

ISBN: 978-1-4185-4404-1

Printed in China

11 12 13 14 15 RRD 8 7 6 5 4

Contents

Foreword   vii

Introduction: Simplicity, A Long-Lost Friend   ix

Discovering That Less Is Truly More   1

1   The Beauty of Simplicity   3

2   The Freedom of Simplicity   9

3   The Joy of Simplicity   15

Embracing Simplicity as a Lifestyle   23

4   Discovering What You Really Need   25

5   Celebrating God Moments   31

6   Taking Time to Reflect   37

Lightening the Load   43

7   Say Farewell to Insecurity   45

8   Letting Go of Unhealthy Patterns   51

9   So Long, Guilt   57

Contents

The Fruit of Simplicity 63

10 Budding with Generosity 65

11 Celebrating with Peace 71

12 Living with Graciousness 77

Leader's Guide 83

Notes 107

About the Author 109

Foreword

My mother ran a tight ship. Loving . . . but tight. When I think back on it, she had dozens of simple four-word homilies we kids called "The Rules." Of course, nothing was set in concrete because mother was a strong believer in grace, but we knew the limits of our liberty.

For example, my two brothers and I often heard phrases like, "Hang up your clothes," "Keep this to yourself," "Pray before you eat," and "Smile when you talk." My favorite injunction was a full sentence she often said to me: "Go find the boys and tell 'em whatever they're doing, quit it." I laugh about it now, but at the time it wasn't funny. When they were unusually quiet, mother instinctively knew "somethin' was *up*," so it was my job to locate the problem and call their hand on it . . . with her blessing, of course.

I distinctly remember one morning when I was fourteen years old. I was getting ready for school when mother instructed me to come straight home that afternoon to help her in the kitchen and set the table for a dinner party she was having at our house that evening. For me to do that, it meant I had to skip volleyball practice and choir rehearsal for a program our chorus was doing the next day. I resented being told what to do by mother, especially since it meant having to miss two of my favorite after-school activities. And I was impertinent, sassy, and annoyed that morning . . . something that was *not allowed* in our home. Nevertheless, I can see it all in my mind now, even though it happened sixty-three years ago. When I got to the front door to leave, mother was sitting on the sofa reading her Bible. I wheeled around, looked back at her, and said with all the flippancy I could muster, "Surely, you don't believe all that stuff, do you, Mother?"

She let just a moment pass, then looked straight at me and said these four words, in the softest, sweetest way possible: "With all my heart." She didn't chide me, yell, put me in my place, or embarrass me in any way. She simply and silently chose a true response and voiced it. And I will never forget those words. Never!

Choosing simplicity is not always easy but the results speak eloquently. Look at these words from Zechariah 8:16 and 17 in *The Message* version of the Bible. The prophet was encouraging his people to honor God, saying, "Here's what I want you to do: Tell the truth, the whole truth, when you speak. Do the right thing by one another, both personally and in your courts. Don't cook up plans to take unfair advantage of others. Don't do or say what isn't so. I hate all that stuff. *Keep your lives simple and honest*" (emphasis mine).

This Bible study guide provides very good direction to finding simplicity in honoring God, as Zechariah suggests. The more we know of His Word, the more we'll want to believe it with all our hearts.

—Luci Swindoll

Introduction

Simplicity, A Long-Lost Friend

It is the sweet, simple things of life
which are the real ones after all.

LAURA INGALLS WILDER,
AUTHOR OF THE *LITTLE HOUSE* BOOK SERIES

Simplicity is like a long-lost friend. When you start spending time with her, you'll find that she helps you see the world with fresh lenses. You'll find delight in areas you've long overlooked. Once you welcome her back into your life, you'll wonder how you ever got along without her.

In our modern world it's easy to get overwhelmed by options, demands, and opportunities. They come at us from every direction, including the places we live, work, and shop. God never intended for us to live feeling stressed or troubled. Irresistible amounts of peace, beauty, and joy can be found in the simplicity of knowing and loving God.

Why is simplicity so essential to our lives? When we choose to embrace simplicity, we discover more margin in our lives for all the good things God wants to give us. We find we have more time for ourselves, our families, and our relationships. When we celebrate simplicity, we can't help slowing down, learning to say no, and drawing healthy boundaries. In the process, we learn to savor life and all its wondrous flavors. We are able to celebrate others' lives and our own. We become more sensitive to those in need and the work that God wants to do in and through us.

My hope and prayer is that throughout this study, you will rediscover the beauty of simplicity, and God will overwhelm you with the simple but powerful message of His love.

Blessings,

Margaret Feinberg

Discovering That Less Is Truly More

*Simplicity is a gift—one that needs to be
unwrapped and enjoyed every day. When we
choose simplicity, we don't have to live with less,
but we discover more of the best things in life.*

One

The Beauty of Simplicity

*To find the air and the water exhilarating; to
be refreshed by a morning walk or an evening
saunter . . . to be thrilled by the stars at night; to be
elated over a bird's nest or a wildflower in spring—
these are some of the rewards of the simple life.*

JOHN BURROUGHS,
AMERICAN LITERARY NATURALIST

Once upon a time, gold fever filled the air. The hope of finding a gold nugget in a nearby stream or mining shaft ignited people's imaginations and dreams. Some moved thousands of miles in pursuit of buried treasure.

Alice had heard stories of men and women who had taken part in the gold rush. Yet she knew better. The odds of finding gold were slim at best.

Content to live at home, Alice spent time working in her garden. In the middle of her yard, she faced her own challenge—a boulder too large to move. Knowing she didn't have the means to remove the stone, she decided to do what she could to make it more beautiful.

She pulled out a piece of sandpaper and began polishing the rock. With enough hard work, the stone would become the centerpiece—a work of beauty—in her garden.

As she worked, Alice began to notice a small line of golden dust collecting on the rock. She pressed her finger on the dust and confirmed—she had found gold. She began sanding harder and faster.

The gold dust accumulated. Her eyes widened. People were traveling far and wide to search for gold; she had discovered it in her own backyard.

She sanded even harder and faster, watching that wealth gather before her eyes.

Alice paused for a moment to catch her breath. That's when she noticed her ring finger felt odd. She looked down. While the top of the ring was fine, the band on the underside was as thin as a thread. She had almost sanded her wedding ring off! All the gold was from her wedding band. Her heirloom had been reduced to dust.

Simplicity helps us recognize the difference between fool's gold and the real treasure.

Alice's story reminds us that we're all susceptible to being fooled. The very things that we treasure most can wear away, erode, and disappear if we're not intentional, careful, and wise. Simplicity helps us recognize the difference between fool's gold and the real treasure.[1]

The beauty of simplicity is that it invites us to slow down and celebrate the priceless wonders that we've already been given in life. Simplicity doesn't want to take anything away from us as much as it wants to give greater appreciation of the good things we already have. Along the way, we discover the invaluable treasures of thankfulness, contentment, and joy.

1. *For Alice, her wedding band was an heirloom and a treasure. What are some things in your life that you treasure?*

2. *Have you given up something you treasured for something that looked like a treasure? If so, describe the occasion.*

3. *In what ways have you discovered that simplicity adds more to your life than it takes away?*

At one point in Israel's history, God gave His people over to the oppressive Midianites because of their disobedience. Gideon, a young man from the small tribe of Manasseh, lived during this time. Gideon's clan was the least remarkable in all of Israel, and Gideon himself was "the least in [his] father's house" (Judges 6:15). Yet God chose to do remarkable things through him. At first, though, Gideon was not very willing to listen to and obey God.

    *4. Read **Judges 6:12–16**. What does this passage say about Gideon's character? How did God view Gideon?*

    5. God was willing to work with Gideon in order to gain his trust. Read the passages and in the chart below fill in the appropriate sign that God gave Gideon.

Scripture Reference	Sign Given by God
Judges 6:17–22	
Judges 6:36–38	
Judges 6:39–40	

God's patience prevailed. Gideon was able to trust God enough to lead his men near the camp of Midian as God had instructed. However, God's plans were very different from what Gideon expected.

6. Read *Judges 7:2–8*. God asked Gideon to cut down the number of his men twice. What was the final number of troops God settled on? What do you think Gideon's reaction was to God's command?

Even though Gideon had fewer soldiers than he'd originally anticipated, God still handed the Midianites over to him and his men.

7. Read *Judges 7:19–22*. At first, Gideon brought along thirty-two thousand men, expecting an epic battle. How did God surprise him? What is your reaction to the end of the story about Gideon and his army?

8. In your own life, where have you seen God make much out of little? How can you change your attitude to allow God to work through simplicity?

When we choose simplicity, we discover that we don't have to live with less but we get to live with more of the best things in life.

Digging Deeper

Read Luke 2:36–38. What was the focus of Anna's life? What was the reward for holding on to this simple commitment of faith in the temple? How have you experienced God's goodness in your own faith journey?

Bonus Activity

Take time away from your normal schedule and spend some time outside, celebrating God's creation. Consider going on a walk or hike. Take time to reflect on the treasures of God's handiwork. Thank Him for making the trees, the animals, the sky, the clouds, and various other things that you see, smell, and feel in nature.

Two

The Freedom of Simplicity

Simplicity is the ultimate sophistication.

LEONARDO DAVINCI,
RENOWNED PAINTER AND INVENTOR

When you're more than nine feet tall, people don't want to mess with you. Most will move out of your way and step aside—no matter the format of confrontation. When your head hits the ceiling in every house you enter, you're a giant, and everyone knows it.

Goliath didn't just tower above his friends; he towered above his enemies. He was a champion among the Philistines, a winner of any battle. Over the years his confidence grew into cockiness as opponents looked for an out, any out, to avoid facing him on the battlefield.

The giant was a master at taunting his opponents. Facing the Israelite army, he challenged them to produce one man to fight him. Then Goliath upped the ante with a high-stakes proposal: if he won, the Israelites would serve the Philistines, but if the opponent won, the Philistines would serve Israel. The proposition terrified the Israelites. No one came forward.

Meanwhile, David, the youngest of eight sons, was busy tending the family's flocks. David's father sent the boy to check on his older brothers, who were fighting against the Philistines, and to take them food. When David arrived on the scene, Goliath was standing in his usual spot and defying Israel's army, begging for someone to fight him.

There are moments in all of our lives when the simplest choice is the best choice.

David announced to King Saul that he would be the one to fight Goliath. When Saul told David that he was not ready—he was only a boy, after all—David shared the stories of his bravery and skill, of killing both a bear and a lion in order to protect his flock. Impressed by the boy's courage and faith in God, Saul permitted David to fight the Philistine, despite the high stakes involved. Saul tried to prepare David for the battle by giving him his own armor and weapons, but the boy rejected them. Instead he went straight to the stream and carefully selected five smooth stones. These—not the king's impressive armaments—would be his weapons.

Though David had access to the latest armor and weaponry, he chose a simple stone and sling for protection. As in David's life, there are moments in all of our lives when the simplest choice is the best choice. Though we may be tempted to choose something more complex or something that doesn't really fit us, when we choose those things that are true to whom God has made us to be, we can't help laying hold of all God has for us.

1. *David and the Israelites faced a giant named Goliath. Most of us will face a giant in our lives at one time or another. What are some of the giants you've faced in the past? How did God prove Himself faithful in those situations?*

2. *What giants are you currently facing? How is God showing Himself to be faithful now?*

David and Goliath took very different approaches when it came to the battle.

3. *Read 1 Samuel 17:4–7 and 1 Samuel 17:38–40. What did Goliath wear and bring to the battle? How does this contrast with what David wore and brought to the battle?*

4. How do you respond when you're facing a giant? What do you reach for to protect yourself?

David and Goliath also took different approaches in what they said when they were about to enter the battle.

5. Read 1 Samuel 17:43–44. Write Goliath's words below.

6. Read 1 Samuel 17:45–47. Write David's words below.

Enraged by David's words, Goliath charged David. David reached into his bag, selected the perfect stone, and placed it in his sling. Then he hurled the rock at his opponent, whacking him in the forehead and killing him instantly.

7. *Who did Goliath consider the source of his expected victory? How does this contrast with who David believed would be the source of his victory?*

8. *What practical steps can you take to remember the simple truth that God is the source of victory in your life?*

When you're facing a giant, it's easy to lose perspective. God invites us to turn to Him, keep our eyes on Him, and remain faithful to Him. This may seem like a simple response, but it's a powerful one.

Digging Deeper

Read **Philippians 4:6–8**. On a scale of 1 to 10 (10 being frequently), how often do you lift your anxieties to God? When you do, do you feel the peace of God, just as Paul described in verse 7? Rewrite verse 8 in the space below. Underline the descriptive words used to express what Paul encouraged us to think about. (Example: whatever is *true*, whatever is *noble*. . . .) Reflect on this passage in the upcoming week.

Bonus Activity

Make a list of your priorities. Place it somewhere you can frequently see, to remind you how you want to spend your money and time. Consider discussing your priority list with a friend so that he or she may help hold you accountable.

Three

The Joy of Simplicity

*Find joy in simplicity, self-respect, and
indifference to what lies between virtue and
vice. Love the human race. Follow the divine.*

MARCUS AURELIUS,
SECOND-CENTURY ROMAN EMPEROR

When we embrace simplicity in different areas of our lives, joy just can't help welling up inside of us. We find new energy and excitement for daily activities. We discover the delight that surrounds us every day—in a child's smile, a friend's hug, a hot cup of cocoa with marshmallows. How much is your joy bubbling up inside of you? Take the Joy Bubble Quiz and find out!

The Joy Bubble Quiz

Circle the answer that best describes you:

1. *Are you feeling confident and fulfilled in your workplace (whether that's home or an office)?*

   Yes   *No*

2. *Do you feel as though God has a purpose for you, and that you're living it out?*

   Yes   *No*

3. *Do feel that you have a community of friends to support you?*

   Yes   *No*

4. *Do you have three things that you're thankful for right now?*

   Yes   *No*

5. *Do you feel as if you have a healthy energy level?*

   Yes   *No*

6. *Do you find that you have enough time in your schedule to pursue at least one of your passions?*

   Yes   *No*

7. *Are you looking forward to the weekend?*

   Yes   *No*

8. *Have you had a hearty laugh in the past two weeks?*

   Yes   *No*

9. *Do you feel that you have more opportunities in your life to get to do something rather than have to do something?*

   Yes   *No*

10. *Do you still remember why you're engaged in the activities in which you're involved?*

    Yes   *No*

Scoring

For every answer that you marked yes, give yourself 3 points. For ever answer you marked no, give yourself 1 point. Total your points and see below:

If you scored 20–30 points, your joy is bubbling over on a regular basis. You are taking time for yourself to enjoy and appreciate where you are in life and what you're doing. You have a knack for keeping your sense of humor, and you know when to let things go. You have a sense of what's truly important, and you embrace God's grace with every step forward.

If you scored 10–19 points, you have room for more joy in your life. Though you know how to celebrate and find delight in the goodness of God, at times you find the busyness of life getting the better of you. No worries! You can still make time to get away and be refreshed. Though it may not always feel like it, sometimes when we choose to do less, God can do so much more through us.

> *Sometimes when we choose to do less, God can do so much more through us.*

No matter what you scored today or this week, know that God wants to fill you with His joy—a kind of joy that wells up from inside of you and is stronger than any challenge you may be facing.

1. When your cup of joy is running low, what kinds of activities fill up your joy cup?

2. How often do you take time to fill up your joy cup? What prevents you from engaging in more activities that leave you content, hopeful, and happy?

One amazing way we can experience more joy in our lives is by knowing and obeying God. The Scriptures invite us to find our delight in God and His Word.

3. When you think of obeying God and His Word, do you think of it adding to your joy or taking away from your joy?

In the first five books of the Old Testament, known as the Torah, more than six hundred commandments are described, but the most famous is found in Deuteronomy 6:4–9—known as the *Shema*. This passage became the basic declaration of faith for Israel in the Old Testament. *Shema* is the Hebrew word for "hear." Read and reflect on the following passage, **Deuteronomy 6:4–9:**

> "Hear, O Israel: The LORD our God, the LORD is one! You shall love the LORD your God with all your heart, with all your soul, and with all your strength. And these words which I command you today

shall be in your heart. You shall teach them diligently to your children, and shall talk of them when you sit in your house, when you walk by the way, when you lie down, and when you rise up. You shall bind them as a sign on your hand, and they shall be as frontlets between your eyes. You shall write them on the doorposts of your house and on your gates."

When these words were spoken to the Israelites, God had already saved them from oppressive slavery in Egypt, led them through the wilderness, and assured them of the promised land. After all God had done for Israel, they were asked to show devotion to Him. The word for love in this passage is *ahava*. This Hebrew word may be translated "to make one's choice in."

4. *Reflecting on* **Deuteronomy 6:5**, *with what are we told to love God? In what ways do you fulfill the* **shema** *in your daily life?*

5. **Deuteronomy 6:6–9** *lists various ways in which you are to remember your devotion to God and His commandments. What are some ways you remember to love Him and keep His commandments?*

The teaching of *Shema* is not just an Old Testament idea. The Gospel of Matthew describes when the Pharisees, who knew that Jesus was familiar with the *Shema*, tried to trip Him up in theological debate. One expert of the Law tested Jesus by asking Him, "Which is the greatest commandment in the Law?" In reply, Jesus referred to the *Shema*. Love God. Love others.

> 6. Read **Matthew 22:34–40**. How did Jesus sum up all of the laws and hang them on these two commandments?

> 7. What are the benefits of loving God and loving others? Look up the following verses and fill in the benefit of following God's commands.

Scripture Reference	Benefit of Following God's Commands
John 14:15–17	(Ex.: *The Holy Spirit will be sent to you*)
1 John 5:3–5	
Joshua 1:8	
Proverbs 10:27	
Deuteronomy 28:1–13	

8. *Describe a time in your life when you experienced joy by doing what Jesus commanded in* **Matthew 22:34–40?**

> *Knowing and obeying God and following*
> *His commands—no matter how simple they*
> *seem—will fill you with joy overflowing.*

Digging Deeper

Jesus tried to make His disciples understand the importance of humility. Read **Matthew 18:1–4.** What's the difference between the child in Jesus' example and the disciples? In your own words, define what it means to have a childlike faith.

Bonus Activity

Choose a day this week to have a Get-the-Couch-off-the-Wall Day. Choose one room in your house, and rearrange the furniture. Recycle or donate any unused items or furniture pieces while you are at it. If you are really feeling adventurous, have an accessory exchange. Take down all the artwork, lamps, pillows, and so forth, and swap them to a different room. A change of scenery may provide for a better, more relaxing living space.

Embracing Simplicity
as a Lifestyle

Simplicity is something we can embrace

in all areas of our lives—our minds,

our schedules, and our hearts.

Four

Discovering What You Really Need

It's easy to be clever. But the really
clever thing is to be simple.

JULE STYNE,
AMERICAN MUSICIAN AND SONGWRITER

Greta was hearing a call in her life—a call to simplicity. After reading various articles and a few books, she knew she needed to fix something about her consumer lifestyle. Greta and her husband, Benji, decided to embark on a journey of anticonsumerism for one year. They made an agreement to not buy any nonconsumable products from January 1 to December 31.

Some of the fine print allowed them to purchase toilet paper and health or safety items. They were also allowed to buy used consumables, just nothing new. Thrift store escapades took the place of heading to the department store or mall. They didn't want to hinder their friends and family with their resolution, so they allowed others to purchase anything for them as gifts.

At the end of August, their microwave broke. By this time, Greta and Benji were ready to give up on the project. They knew they couldn't keep going with just the stovetop oven for the rest of the year. Buying a used microwave was going to cost more than buying a new one.

That night they were surprised by someone at their door. As they got up to answer the door, they heard a car speed off. On their front porch they discovered a brand-new microwave. One of their friends decided to bless them with the gift.

Living simply does more than just help to save money . . . a simple lifestyle can also infuse us with the energy to live out our love of God and meet the needs of others.

Though their yearlong commitment is over now, they know the experience has made an impact on their lives. They've returned to buying new things, but they say they're much more aware of the reasons behind their purchase. Are they making a purchase because they had a bad day? Because they want to impress someone? Because they need to save time? Instead of being impulsive, they're finding themselves in the habit of taking a step back and evaluating the true meaning and purpose behind their purchases.

The "Buy Nothing New" year began after both Greta and Benji finished graduate school—leaving them with student loans to pay off. Not only did this year aid them spiritually, but by December the couple were able to pay off all of their college debt with the money they saved. Though they're grateful for that, they are even more thankful for the work that was done in their hearts over the course of the year. They discovered that living simply does more than just help to save money or add to a retirement fund; a simple lifestyle can also infuse us with the energy to live out our love of God and meet the needs of others.

1. *Would you ever consider this "Buy Nothing New" lifestyle for a week? A month? A year? What would concern you about the experiment? What would excite you?*

2. *Greta and Benji recognized that they purchased things for a variety of reasons. Sometimes they needed something, but other times they were responding to a bad day or hoping to impress someone. What motivates your shopping?*

3. *Take a few moments and walk into a main room in your house. In the table below, list all the physical items you see.*

(Ex.: Television)		

4. Circle the items you listed in the table on page 27 that are essential for everyday life.

5. What did the exercise reveal about the amount of things in your life?

While we may not always be able to identify exactly what we need, God knows. Referred to as the Lord's Prayer, Matthew 6:9–13 highlights our dependence on God for all our needs.

*6. Read **Matthew 6:9–13**, focusing on verse 11. What did Jesus say we should ask for?*

This reference to food is symbolic. We should ask God to not only meet our physical needs but also our spiritual ones. This alludes to the time when the Israelites were wandering in the desert after God freed them from slavery in Egypt. In Exodus 16, God met their needs by providing bread from heaven. The bread is later named *manna*.

7. What are some of your "manna needs"—those things that only God can provide for you?

8. How often do you ask God for what you need as encouraged in the Lord's Prayer? Does anything prevent you from being fully honest with God about your needs? Explain.

Jesus promises to meet all of our needs, but not all of our wants.

Digging Deeper

David wrote Psalm 23 reflecting on the metaphor of God as the Good Shepherd who cares for His sheep. Reflect on **Psalm 23:1**. Read this verse at least three times out loud. Some translations of the verse replace "I shall not want" with "I am lacking nothing." What does it feel like to be lacking nothing? How would your attitude change if you placed all your trust in God to provide for your needs?

Bonus Activity

One of the books Greta read that sparked this journey was *Freedom of Simplicity* by Richard J. Foster (HarperOne, 2005). Consider checking this out from your local library to see what changes you can make in the journey toward simplicity.

Five

Celebrating God Moments

I would rather walk with God in the
dark than go alone in the light.

MARY GARDINER BRAINARD,
AMERICAN RELIGIOUS POET

Cartoons from the *The New Yorker* are known for being smart, engaging, and funny. A recent issue featured a scene with two couples in the grocery store. The couples are heading in opposite directions, shopping carts full. Looking over their shoulders, one couple says to the other, "You're on our 'to do' list." Everyone pictured is smiling, communicating ease and calmness. Yet the scene highlights the irony that while people may want to get together, they don't have the time to even plan it.[1]

Most of us live with to-do lists. They include activities, projects, and even people. Like the couples portrayed in the cartoon, we may see something or someone and be reminded that we have a long-lost friend with whom we really need to get back in touch, a family member that we need to check in with, or a loved one that we need to reach out to. Yet the busyness of life can prevent us from cherishing and celebrating these relationships as much as we desire.

One relationship that was never meant to go on a to-do list is our relationship with God. He is so much more than a to-do! God is a delight and a joy. He is a source of strength, hope, and love. No matter how busy life may get, He always has time for you.

Even when your to-do list seems miles long, God still desires a relationship with you. He wants to be with you. Express His love for you. Draw you closer to Him. These "God moments" are precious and can happen anytime, anywhere. You may be driving around town, running errands, when a worship song on the radio ushers you into a time of personal worship with God. You may be standing in a long checkout line when you're reminded to pray for someone in need. You may be preparing a meal when someone you have the means to help crosses your mind.

> *No matter how busy life may get, God always has time for you. Even when your to-do list seems miles long, God still desires a relationship with you.*

How do you celebrate a "God moment"? By responding to the opportunity. Take time to praise. Take time to pray. Take time to demonstrate God's love to others. And in the process, you just might discover that you get more done that you ever imagined.

1. *Think about your current to-do list. How many items are on it? Which are the most pressing? Which items do you tend to push toward the bottom of the list?*

2. With whom do you need to reconnect or make time to get together this week? What's stopping you from making the time?

3. When was the last "God moment"—a time when God made Himself real to you—that you encountered? What happened?

4. Have you noticed a pattern in the times when God is most likely to get your attention and draw your heart back to His own? Explain.

The "God moments" in our lives often catch us by surprise. We may be busy getting our chores done or taking care of the task at hand when God surprises us with Himself. In Luke 24, three different groups of people encounter some unexpected God moments as they're going about their to-do lists and life.

5. Read *Luke 24:1–12*. *What were the women busy doing (v. 1)? How did God surprise them (vv. 4–7)? How do you think you would have responded to the "God moment"?*

6. Read *Luke 24:13–35*. *What were the two men busy doing (v. 13)? How did God surprise them (vv. 14–35)?*

7. Read *Luke 24:36–53*. *What were the disciples busy doing (v. 36)? How did God surprise them (vv. 36–51)?*

While not all of our God moments are as spectacular as those displayed in Luke 24, God still makes Himself real to each of us today in His own way.

8. *What can you do to make yourself more open and available to God moments in your daily life?*

God has a way of surprising us with Himself. Keep your eyes, ears, and hearts open to the God moments when He wants to reveal Himself to you.

Digging Deeper

We may think we're too old or somehow disqualified from having a profound encounter with God, but nothing could be farther from the truth. God has a way of revealing Himself in amazing and profound ways. Read **Genesis 17**. How old was Abram when he had a profound God moment? How did it shape and change the course of His life? Why do you think God reveals Himself to people in so many different ways and calls them to so many different things? What do you think God is calling you to right now? In what ways was the message given to Abraham and the journey he made meaningful to you?

Bonus Activity

Create a "God Moment" journal. Select an old notebook and consider decorating it with paints, markers, beads, or other colorful artwork. Whenever you encounter a God moment—no matter how small it may seem—write it in your journal and reflect on the work God is doing in your life.

Six

Taking Time to Reflect

*Frequent combing gives the hair more luster
and makes it easier to comb; a soul that
frequently examines its thoughts, words, and
deeds, which are its hair, doing all things for
the love of God, will have lustrous hair.*

JOHN OF THE CROSS,
SIXTEENTH-CENTURY PRIEST AND FRIAR

In the Greek culture, people know that time is something to be treasured and enjoyed. Maybe that's one reason the Greeks actually have two different words or expressions for "time." The first word is *chronos*, and it's the word meaning "of time that is attached to a clock and calendar." This type of time can be counted and measured with precision. Minutes and hours and days and weeks mark the *chronos*, or chronological passing of time.

But the ancient Greeks recognized another aspect of time—an expression that celebrated time as a gift to be savored. The second Greek word for time is *kairos*. The word doesn't express a measurement of time as much as the potential contained within the moment.

While *chronos* may ask the question, "What season are we in?" *kairos* asks, "How can we make the most out of this season of life?" The difference is subtle but significant.

> *God was the first one to take the Sabbath—the seventh day of creation—to rest. He did so as an example for all of us.*

Chronos asks us to pay attention to our day planners; *kairos* invites us to pack our days with potential—joy, hope, rest, and laughter. While *chronos* reminds us that the deadline is approaching, *kairos* encourages us to put our very best into the project. *Chronos* urges us to check our watches, but *kairos* asks us to enjoy the vistas of life and the wonders that fill our every day.

We all are given the same *chronos*, or measurement of time, each day, but what are we doing with it? How are we making the most of it? How much of it are we really celebrating?

What's amazing is that simply by changing our perspective we can turn *chronos* moments into *kairos* moments. Though our time may be full of commitments, we can learn to appreciate the beauty and wonder along the way. We can learn to slow down and enjoy every moment more. We can learn to savor more of life.

1. In the space below, make a list of three chronos *activities, and then make a list of three* kairos *activities.*

2. *Do you feel as though you spend more of your life in* **chronos** *or* **kairos** *moments? Explain.*

3. *What changes in your life would lead to experiencing more* **kairos** *moments?*

Sometimes taking time away to reflect or taking a day off may seem countercultural, but it's a culture and a pattern that actually began with God. God was the first one to take the Sabbath—the seventh day of creation—to rest. He did so as an example for all of us.

4. *Read* **Genesis 2:2–3**. *Why do you think God took a day to rest?*

The importance of God's choice to rest on the seventh day was highly significant to the people of Israel. After serving in slavery to the Egyptians, God finally set His people free and gave them a new leader named Moses. While on Mount Sinai, God gave Moses the Ten Commandments, which begin with the words "I am the LORD your God, who brought you out of the land of Egypt, out of the house of bondage" (Exodus 20:2). In essence, God was saying that the Israelites may have lived one way under the rule of Pharaoh, but they were now being called to live another way as the people of God.

5. Read **Exodus 20:1–17**. Why do you think remembering the Sabbath is one of the Ten Commandments? Do you think this command is as important as not murdering or stealing or worshipping other gods? Why or why not?

Though God made it clear that keeping the Sabbath is important, Jesus suggested that keeping the Sabbath should not keep us from loving others more; it actually *empowers* us to love them more.

6. Read **Matthew 12:1–14**. What were the Pharisees' concerns regarding the Sabbath (v. 2)? Do you think they were justified in their response? Why or why not?

7. What was Jesus' response to the Pharisees (vv. 3–14)? Why do you think Jesus didn't just answer their concern but also went on to heal the man on the Sabbath?

8. When it comes to taking a day off or making time to reflect, what practices are the most effective for you? How do you plan for times of rest and reflection? How do these times help you simplify your life?

When we choose to reflect on life, we get a chance to gain a healthy perspective, sort through priorities, and make the most of life. We move from passing the time in chronos *moments to truly living a* kairos *life.*

Digging Deeper

Read Isaiah 58:13–14. In what ways have you found the Sabbath to be a delight? What are some of the specific rewards of the Sabbath that you've discovered? How does a day of rest increase your joy? How does your perspective on life and priorities change? What prevents you from taking more time to rest and get away?

Bonus Activity

Take a few moments to reflect on your calendar. On a piece of paper, either write out or print out your schedule for the upcoming week. Mark each activity with the either the word *chronos* or the word *kairos*, based on whether it's something that merely fills your time, or that fills you with life. Prayerfully reflect on how you can transform some of your *chronos* moments into *kairos* moments.

Lightening
the Load

*Sometimes we carry around things that
weigh us down and prevent us from
enjoying the simplicity of our faith.*

Seven

Say Farewell to Insecurity

We could avoid most of our problems if we
only learned how to sit quietly in our room.

BLAISE PASCAL,
SEVENTEENTH-CENTURY MATHEMATICIAN AND PHILOSOPHER

The 1996 Summer Olympic Games were celebrated in Atlanta, Georgia. Like thousands of athletes, Jonathan wondered if he had what it took—especially when it came to the triple jump. Despite his success at previous international competitions, the media questioned his ability to perform. Did he still have what it took to compete under the Olympic spotlight? The headlines fed the young athlete's own doubts and insecurities.

As the event approached, one thought from the apostle Peter kept the athlete steady: "In this you greatly rejoice, though now for a little while you may have had to suffer grief in all kinds of trials. These have come so that your faith—of greater worth than gold, which perishes even though refined by fire—may be proved genuine and may result in praise, glory and honor when Jesus Christ is revealed" (1 Peter 1:6–7 NIV).

After the competition, Jonathan stood proudly on the podium, wearing a bronze medal. Four years later, at the 2000 Summer Olympics, he came home with the gold.[1] While most of us don't have to face the intense pressure that comes with being an Olympic athlete, we still face daily pressures and situations that bring our insecurities to the surface. Most of us are all too familiar with our weaknesses and the areas where we feel we can't compete or don't measure up. But we don't have to listen to the critics—especially when the critic is ourselves. We can choose to listen to what God has to say about us and the promises that He makes to us.

You will face challenges in life that will test your faith, but you don't have to let your doubts, fears, and insecurities get the best of you.

You will face challenges in life that will test your faith, but you don't have to let your doubts, fears, and insecurities get the best of you. Say farewell to everything that holds you back—and hello to everything God has for you.

1. *In what ways do our insecurities make our lives and relationships more complex than they need to be?*

2. *What types of situations tend to make you feel the most insecure?*

3. *How do you deal with insecurities in your own life? How do you tend to respond?*

One of the heaviest things many of us carry around is insecurity. It makes our relationships and lives more complex than they need to be. When we say farewell to insecurity, we'll find our minds are decluttered, our relationships are more fulfilling, and we can't help living with a little more bounce.

4. *Read* **Psalm 139:1–18**. *The Hebrew word for* **searched** *(v. 1) can be translated "investigated." How does it make you feel to know that God knows you so intimately?*

5. *Do you believe that you are "fearfully and wonderfully made" (v. 14)? Why or why not? Why is it important to know that God did good work when He made you? How does this change your perspective on life? Others? Yourself?*

Psalm 91, a psalm of trust, does not state its author. This well-known psalm describes the intimate relationship between God and those who trust in Him.

6. Read **Psalm 91**. *When you're facing insecurity, what kind of comfort and strength can you find in this psalm?*

7. *Look up the following passages, and write them out next to each entry:*

Scripture Reference	Scripture
Psalm 56:3–4	
Isaiah 41:10	
John 14:1	
John 16:33	

8. *Which of these passages (or others) are the most encouraging to you when you think about insecurities in your life?*

Simplifying our lives means dealing with the things—both tangible and intangible—that weigh us down, including insecurities.

Digging Deeper

Instead of living with insecurity, God wants us to live with His peace flooding our lives. Read **Philippians 2:1–11**. What does it look like to imitate Christ in our lives? Have you ever noticed that your own insecurities disappear when your focus is on building someone else up? Describe.

Bonus Activity

Write the words of **Galatians 5:1** on multiple note cards. Place them around your house, bathroom, car, or office. Allow this Scripture to be a constant reminder of the importance of keeping the freedom God has for you.

Eight

Letting Go of Unhealthy Patterns

The sculptor produces the beautiful statue by
chipping away such parts of the marble block as
are not needed—it is a process of elimination.

ELBERT HUBBARD,
AMERICAN WRITER AND PHILOSOPHER

J. Sidlow Baxter, twentieth-century theologian and author of more than thirty books, was a very busy preacher, ministering not only in his own church as pastor, but in other churches, Bible conferences, and missions centers around the world. One day, at a meeting of pastors, one man asked Baxter about his prayer life. What did it look like? How did he maintain a vibrant prayer life with so many daily demands?

Baxter explained that when he entered the ministry, he was committed to being a man of prayer. He wanted to pray regularly, faithfully, and tenaciously. But it wasn't long until he began to feel the pressures of everyday life stack up. His schedule filled until no margin was left. People from his congregation were in need, and he responded. The demands of pastoral life were crowding out his prayer life. He began making small justifications—the needs at hand were too great.

One morning he walked into his office and stood in front of his desk overflowing with projects and paperwork. He looked at his watch. He sensed God's spirit welcoming him into a time of prayer. But he also sensed another source suggesting that he simply wasn't a "spiritual sort," and only a few people could be like that. Baxter quickly came to his senses. He realized that he was rationalizing away prayer—the very source of his connection and relationship with God. The moment became a turning point for Baxter and a reminder that while prayer increases the possibilities, lack of prayer only increases the impossibilities.[1]

> *It's never too late to run into the arms of our loving God.*

Like Baxter, all of us have moments when we realize that we've let go of healthy patterns and replaced them with unhealthy ones. In the busyness of life, we may unintentionally give up times of personal prayer, Bible study, connecting with others who love Jesus, or a list of activities that help us stay connected to God and one another. The good news is that unhealthy patterns don't have to get the best of us. We can make choices to embrace the life God intends for us—one filled with joy, hope, peace, and love.

It's never too late to run into the arms of our loving God.

1. *In what ways can you relate to Baxter's story of struggling to make time to pray? Explain.*

2. *When you think of the healthy patterns in your life, do you tend to fall into them by accident or do they require you to be intentional? Explain.*

3. *When you think of the unhealthy patterns in your life, do you tend to fall into them by accident or do they also require you to be intentional? Explain.*

Luke 19 tells of a man who becomes susceptible to some bad choices that were not just affecting himself but everyone he worked with. Zacchaeus was a tax collector, but rather than collect the appropriate amount of taxes, he charged extra to pad his own pockets. While we'll never know exactly what went through Zacchaeus's mind, he may have justified the unhealthy decision by telling himself that he was only asking for a *little* bit extra and from just one or two people. But before he knew it, he was demanding extra money from everyone.

*4. Read **Luke 19:1–10**. What was Jesus' comment to Zacchaeus (v. 5)? What were the people's responses to the scene (v. 7)?*

Zacchaeus's name means "pure" or "clean." When Jesus greeted Zacchaeus, He did so by name (v. 5). Though Zacchaeus was corrupt and had unhealthy patterns in his life, Jesus knew it was not too late. Zacchaeus could repent and change his ways. It's interesting to note that Jesus never asked Zacchaeus to make any changes in his life. Zacchaeus offered to make the changes on his own.

5. What was Zacchaeus's response to Jesus (vv. 6 and 8)?

*6. In the previous chapter in Luke, another rich man encountered Jesus, but the results were not the same. Read **Luke 18:18–29**. What was Jesus' response to the rich ruler (vv. 19–22)?*

7. *How did the rich ruler's response to Jesus differ from Zacchaeus's (v. 23)?*

Both the rich ruler and Zacchaeus had unhealthy patterns and perspectives regarding money in their lives that were highlighted when they encountered Jesus. Both responded in different ways.

8. *How do you respond when you recognize that you have an unhealthy pattern or perspective in your life? What can you do to be more responsive to the work God wants to do you in your life?*

Sometimes we lose simplicity when unhealthy patterns appear in our lives. God wants us to experience freedom and wholeness in every area of our lives.

Digging Deeper

People who encounter Jesus never leave the same. Read John 8:1–11. What emotions do you think the woman in this passage felt? What did Jesus tell her to do with the unhealthy patterns in her life? Do you think the change was easy or hard for the woman? Think of a time when you made a healthy change in your life. What made the difference in letting go of the unhealthy patterns?

Bonus Activity

Over the course of the week, commit Psalm 103:2–5 (NIV) to memory: "Praise the LORD, O my soul, and forget not all his benefits—who forgives all your sins and heals all your diseases, who redeems your life from the pit and crowns you with love and compassion, who satisfies your desires with good things so that your youth is renewed like the eagle's."

Nine

So Long, Guilt

*If you cultivate a healthy poverty and
simplicity, so that finding a penny will literally
make your day, then, since the world is in
fact planted in pennies, you will have with
your poverty bought a lifetime of days.*

ANNIE DILLARD,
PULITZER PRIZE—WINNING AUTHOR

As a young monk, Martin Luther was known for exasperating those to whom he confessed his sins within the monastery. He spent as many as six hours straight confessing minuscule sins, unhealthy thoughts, and the guilt he felt from doing various daily activities. Luther finally realized that his fear of sinning was preventing him from growing in his faith and trusting God.

While it's easy to look at someone like Martin Luther and see how guilt was holding him back in his own journey, sometimes it's harder to recognize how guilt holds us back in our own lives. At times, all of us will feel guilty. We may have done something wrong or left something undone. Guilt is what we experience afterward.

Guilt usually has two parts—the actual offense and the emotions you feel.

The good news is that guilt, or the moment we feel remorseful, can compel us to make things right. We may feel remorseful about an unkind word we said, and the guilt compels us to go and apologize, bringing healing to the relationship. We may feel guilty about something that we damaged or took without asking, and the remorse compels us to go back and pay restitution to the owner. Healthy guilt is a God-given emotion that motivates us to walk in wholeness in all of our relationships—including our relationship with God. When we ask God to forgive us for something we've done or left undone, He is faithful to do so. Though our emotions may try to tell us otherwise, our sin is as good as gone in God's eyes.

> *When we ask God to forgive us for something we've done or left undone . . . our sin is as good as gone in God's eyes.*

Our lives become so much simpler when we let go of guilt and recognize that when we confess our sins and change our ways, God is faithful to forgive us. God doesn't want us to walk around with the burden of guilt but in the fullness of the freedom and forgiveness He offers.

1. *What kinds of situations cause you to feel guilty? How do you tend to respond to guilt?*

2. When you ask **a friend or relative** *to forgive you for something you've done, do you feel guilt-free afterward? Why or why not?*

3. When you ask **God** *to forgive you for something you've done, do you feel guilt-free afterward? Why or why not?*

4. Read **Psalm 38:4**. *How does this passage describe guilt? What words would you use to describe guilt?*

*5. Read **Psalm 32**. How did David respond to the sin in his life? What was God's response to David's confession and repentance?*

Though we may be tempted to carry around guilt, God made it clear throughout the Bible that if we confess to Him what we've done wrong, *He will* forgive us. Through the work of Jesus, God cleanses us of all sin and invites us to live in freedom.

6. In the following chart, match up the Scripture reference to the passage.

Scripture Reference	Passage
Matthew 6:14	"And be kind to one another, tenderhearted, forgiving one another, even as God in Christ forgave you."
Acts 5:31	"Him God has exalted to His right hand to be Prince and Savior, to give repentance to Israel and forgiveness of sins."
Ephesians 1:7	"If we confess our sins, He is faithful and just to forgive us our sins and to cleanse us from all unrighteousness."
1 John 1:9	"For if you forgive men their trespasses, your heavenly Father will also forgive you."
Ephesians 4:32	"Bearing with one another, and forgiving one another, if anyone has a complaint against another; even as Christ forgave you, so you also must do."
Colossians 3:13	"In Him we have redemption through His blood, the forgiveness of sins, according to the riches of His grace."

7. *Reflecting on the Scriptures in the chart in question 6, what comfort do you find in the passages?*

8. *Are there any areas in your life where you're hanging on to unhealthy guilt when it's time to let go? What steps do you need to take to move beyond the guilt and into the grace God has for you?*

Guilt is one of the heaviest pieces of baggage we can try to carry around. God doesn't want us to feel guilty but to experience the freedom and forgiveness He offers.

Digging Deeper

Read **John 1:19–34.** How did John the Baptist describe Jesus in verse 29? Why is this significant to us? Do you see Jesus as the One who takes away your sin? Why or why not? How does knowing that Jesus offers forgiveness empower you to love and serve Him more?

Bonus Activity

Sometimes the hardest person to forgive is yourself. Prayerfully consider if there are any things for which you've had a hard time forgiving yourself. Write them down on a piece of paper. Ask God to forgive you. Now choose to forgive yourself. As a sign of forgiveness, take the sheet of paper and shred it into dozens of pieces. Allow the exercise to remind you that you truly are forgiven.

The Fruit
of Simplicity

Not only does simplicity provide joy and freedom; it also allows us to use our time and treasure in more fruitful, generous ways.

Ten

Budding with Generosity

Nothing is really ours until we share it.

C. S. Lewis,
British novelist and apologist

In the scorching heat, an immigrant named Elijah walked to the small town of Zarephath. As he reached the town's gates, he spotted a woman gathering sticks and twigs. Elijah remembered what the Lord had commanded him: *Go to Zarephath and stay there. A widow will supply you with food.* Elijah cleared his parched throat and called to the woman at the gate.

"Please give me a drink."

The widow responded with kindness and generosity. She did not hesitate to show the stranger hospitality. She turned to get the visitor some water when she heard his voice a second time: "Please bring me a piece of bread."

The widow felt a wave of anguish crash over her. Didn't the stranger know? Famine was widespread throughout the land. The woman and her son hadn't eaten a full meal in as long as she could remember. While she wanted to show the man generosity, she could not give what she did not have.

"I have no bread," she explained. "Only a handful of flour and a little oil." She then admitted that the only reason she was gathering a few sticks was to start a fire so she and her son could enjoy their final meal together before they died.

God is not concerned with the size of the gift as much as the heart behind the gift.

Elijah could sense the despair in her voice, but he didn't flinch. Instead, he encouraged her with the words, "Do not fear!" Confident in God, Elijah instructed the widow to make two loaves of bread—one for him and the other for the woman and her son. He promised that God would ensure that neither flour nor oil would run out until the famine ended.

The woman accepted the invitation of faith. She made a loaf for the prophet, then another for her and her son. Miraculously, she had plenty of flour and oil for their first meal together and many meals afterward. Just as the prophet had promised, the bread and oil didn't run out.

The story of the widow at Zarephath, found in 1 Kings 17, is a beautiful example of generosity. Though what she had to offer the prophet was simple—water and bread—God used her small gifts and hospitality to demonstrate His faithfulness and provision. The widow's kindness reminds us that you don't need something elaborate or fancy for God to work something amazing through you.

1. *Read 1 Kings 17:8–16. What surprises you most about Elijah's encounter with the widow?*

2. *Have you ever been asked to give something that was a stretch for you to give? What was the result?*

3. *What kinds of things are naturally easy for you to give? What kinds of things are more difficult?*

It's easy to think that generosity means giving big gifts, but God is not concerned with the size of the gift as much as the heart behind the gift. In Mark 12, a widow offered a simple gift to God—two thin coins. Yet Jesus celebrated her gift in a story that's been retold countless times.

4. *Read **Mark 12:41–44**. What was moving to Jesus about the widow's gift?*

5. *What makes a gift truly meaningful in your eyes? What makes a gift truly meaningful in God's eyes?*

6. *God makes rich promises to those who are generous. In the following chart, match the Scripture reference to the passage.*

Scripture Reference	Passage
Psalm 41:1	"The generous soul will be made rich, And he who waters will also be watered himself."
Proverbs 3:9–10	"If you extend your soul to the hungry, and satisfy the afflicted soul, then your light shall dawn in the darkness, and your darkness shall be as the noonday."
Proverbs 11:25	"Blessed is he who considers the poor; The LORD will deliver him in time of trouble."
Isaiah 58:10	"Honor the LORD with your possessions, and with the firstfruits of all your increase; So your barns will be filled with plenty, and your vats will overflow with new wine."

7. *Reflecting on the Scriptures in the chart on page 68, how have you found these promises of God to be true in your own life?*

8. *What are some of the specific joys you've experienced through giving and generosity?*

> *Gifts don't have to be complex to be generous expressions of our love for God and others. Sometimes the simplest gift is the most meaningful.*

Digging Deeper

In the Old Testament, generosity sprang forth when it came to the building of the tabernacle. Read **Exodus 36:2–7**. Have you ever been part of a giving situation where there was more than enough? Describe. Why do you think God used the gifts of everyone to build the tabernacle and not just one person? Why is it important for each person to give as he or she is able?

Bonus Activity

Over the course of the next week, pay special attention to those around you who may express a need. You may notice that a friend needs some help painting or getting something small fixed. As an act of kindness and generosity, help meet that need in a thoughtful way.

Eleven

Celebrating with Peace

All works of love are works of peace.

MOTHER TERESA OF CALCUTTA
(1910–97)

A wealthy man wanted a masterpiece for his home. As he considered various images and ideas, he realized that more than anything, he wanted the perfect picture of peace. He traveled from town to town, searching among art galleries and local artists. Frustrated that he couldn't find exactly what he was looking for, he decided to host a contest.

Word quickly spread of the competition. Artists of all genres submitted their work. A team of judges sorted through the entries until two portraits were considered the finalists.

In front of a crowded room, the first picture was unveiled. Gasps filled the air. The portrait revealed a crystal-smooth lake reflecting the surrounding landscape and pale evening sky. The grassy shore was lined with sheep grazing on fresh grass.

The audience erupted in applause. Then all eyes turned to the second piece of art. When the image was unveiled, silence filled the room. The portrait revealed a rocky cliff with a narrow waterfall crawling down the dangerous mountainside. Overhead, ominous storm clouds filled the air. Halfway down the cliff, a single scraggly tree grasped onto the rocky face. On its sole branch, a bird had built a nest and was resting atop her eggs. The bird's eyes were closed, and the small creature portrayed a peace that transcended all the surrounding difficulty.[1]

Whether life is simple and straightforward or complex and confusing, God's peace is available.

Which portrait best represented peace?

Both artists captured an image of peace. While peace can be found in absence of conflict or difficulty, peace can also be found in the midst of challenges and hardship. While almost everyone would prefer a glassy lake on a calm day to a rocky mountainside perched in calamity, God's peace can be found no matter what the situation. Whether life is simple and straightforward or complex and confusing, God's peace is available to us.

1. *Which of the two portraits best describes your life right now? Explain.*

2. *When you think of God's peace, do you tend to think of the scene at the lake or the scene at the cliff? Why?*

3. *Describe a time in your life when you experienced God's peace as the scene at the lake. Describe a time in your life when you experienced God's peace as the scene at the cliff.*

The apostle Paul was a mentor and friend to Timothy. The letters he wrote to the young man were filled with words of encouragement, and they challenged him to grow in his faith and knowledge of Jesus. In 1 Timothy 6, Paul gave some specific instructions to Timothy.

4. *Read **1 Timothy 6:11–16**. What instruction did Paul give to Timothy? Do you think Paul believed that Timothy's journey would be easy? Why or why not?*

5. *What do you think Paul meant when he said, "Fight the good fight of faith" (v. 12)? Do you think it's possible to "fight the good fight" and still maintain peace in your heart? Why or why not?*

Before Jesus was arrested and killed, He spent some precious time with His followers, teaching them all kinds of spiritual lessons. In John 14, Jesus told His disciples what was going to happen to Him and to them.

6. Read **John 14:15–31**. What did Jesus tell the disciples that He was going to give them (vv. 25–27)?

7. Why do you think Jesus clarified that His peace is different from the world's peace? How is the peace that Jesus gives different from the peace that the world gives?

8. When in your life have you seen the peace that the world gives? That Jesus gives?

God provides peace—a kind of peace that floods
our hearts and lives with contentment despite
what may be going on around us.

Digging Deeper

Peace is one of the fruits of the Spirit. Read **Galatians 5:16–26**. What
are some of the activities mentioned in this passage that prevent us
from experiencing the peace God wants to give us? What are the
fruits of the Spirit? How are these fruits growing in your life right
now?

Bonus Activity

Set aside time this week to paint or draw. Using whatever canvas or
paper you choose, illustrate a picture embodying the peace of Christ.
Consider writing a verse from John 14 on your artwork.

Twelve

Living with Graciousness

*If there is any singular truth that distinguishes
Christianity from all other religions, all
other systems of belief, it is grace.*

CHARLES R. SWINDOLL,
BEST-SELLING AUTHOR AND PASTOR OF
STONEBRIAR COMMUNITY CHURCH

A popular fish among many in Japan is the carp, also known as the koi. These fish have an unusual quality. If you place a koi in a glass fish bowl, it will only grow to be two to three inches long. If you take that same fish and place it in a larger fish tank, the length of the koi will reach six to ten inches. If you take the same koi and place it in a large outdoor pond, the fish will grow up to a foot-and-a-half in length. But if you take a koi and release it into a lake where it can swim freely, it can grow up to three feet long.[1]

Like the koi, all of us have incredible potential when it comes to growing in God and expressing His love and goodness to others. Though we may think we are at full capacity, God has a way of expanding our horizons so we can grow into the fullness of all He has for us and all He has created us to be.

Growing in God often requires placing ourselves in situations that are new, different, and challenging. Sometimes we sign up for these opportunities. Others times we find ourselves in them.

The littlest and simplest acts can make the biggest difference in our lives—and the lives of those we love.

The fruit of simplicity is that we have more time to be kind, respond to small needs, and honor others above ourselves. We may find ourselves working alongside someone with whom we don't naturally get along, yet the opportunity gives us a chance to practice kindness and gentleness. We may discover that a friend we care about has become sick, and we are given the opportunity to grow in compassion and service. We may find ourselves in a situation where someone has wronged us and we learn that with God's help we can expand our heart to forgive. Along the way we discover that the littlest and simplest acts can make the biggest difference in our lives—and the lives of those we love.

1. In what ways do you feel that God has been growing you over the last few months?

2. What kinds of situations encourage you to extend God's grace to others?

God demonstrates compassion and graciousness in the way that He responds to us. Throughout the Scriptures, we are reminded that we serve a loving and good God.

3. Look up the following passages. Next to each Scripture reference write the words used in the passage to describe God.

Psalm 86:15:

Psalm 103:8:

Psalm 111:4:

4. How does knowing that God is compassionate and gracious encourage you to be compassionate and gracious with others? What types of situations make it the most difficult for you to show compassion and grace? According to these passages, how would God respond to these situations?

5. Read **Romans 12:1–8**. *According to this passage, what are some of the hallmarks of being a child of God? What are we called to do as children of God (vv. 6–8)?*

6. *Of the gifts mentioned in* **Romans 12:6–8**, *which do you feel that God has given you? How does using your gifts allow you to experience and share the grace of God with others? How has using your gifts allowed you to grow as a person?*

7. Read **Romans 12:9–21**. *Does anything surprise you about Paul's instruction to believers? What do you think makes being a follower of Jesus so simple? What do you think makes it complex?*

8. *What areas of your life do you feel God inviting you to simplify so that you can grow in Him even more?*

The fruit of simplicity is that you have more margin to take time to be kind, respond to needs, and honor others above yourself. In the process, you'll find yourself growing in ways you never imagined.

Digging Deeper

Jesus made it clear that when we are gracious and generous with others, we aren't to tell everyone about it. We are to work for God, instead of the applause of others. Read **Matthew 6:1–4**. In what ways does following Jesus' instruction simplify acts of graciousness and generosity? How does it make you feel to know that God rewards you for your work? Are there any situations in which you'd rather receive a reward from others than from God? Explain.

Bonus Activity

Spend an afternoon this week volunteering. You may want to visit a local hospital, nursing home, or food bank. Look for a specific opportunity to extend God's grace and care to others.

Leader's Guide

Chapter 1: The Beauty of Simplicity

Focus: *When we choose simplicity, we discover that we don't have to live with less, but we get to live with more of the best things in life.*

1. *Answers will vary. Encourage participants to share some of things they celebrate and enjoy in life. Note that many of the things we treasure in life are things that money can't buy, like our families, our relationships, and our loved ones.*

2. *As a leader, it may help to have a story from your own life to share with the group. Some examples may include your experience with using a "time-saving" device that actually cost you more time, placing expectations on someone that were too high for that person to live up to, or letting go of valued friendships because of the busyness of life.*

3. *Answers will vary. Encourage participants to think about different areas of life and explore the idea that less can really be a whole lot more.*

4. *Gideon seemed to be cynical, fearful, and hesitant. He criticized God and His treatment of Israel. He didn't feel worthy or useful in God's plan. God viewed Gideon as a "mighty man of valor" (v. 12). He was confident in Gideon's usefulness and knew that through him, He would strike down the Midianites.*

5. *Answers:*

Scripture Reference	Sign Given by God
Judges 6:17–22	The angel of the Lord consumed the meat and bread of Gideon's sacrifice after touching it with his staff.
Judges 6:36–38	God made the fleece wet, while keeping the ground beneath it dry.
Judges 6:39–40	God reversed His last miracle by keeping the fleece dry and having the ground beneath it wet.

6. *God allowed Gideon to keep three hundred men. At first, Gideon may have questioned or doubted God, but despite what Gideon may have felt, he chose to obey God and cut down the number of his men significantly.*

7. *Instead of battle, Gideon and his army simply scared the Midianites. Then God had the Midianites turn against one another. Answers will vary, but this story is a powerful reminder that God can do a lot with just a little. There are no limits with a God as big as ours. For some, this may be surprising; for others, comforting.*

8. *Answers will vary. Some participants may not have a great story to tell, like Gideon's. But God can do amazing things with small amounts of people, time, money, and love. By allowing ourselves to trust God, we allow Him opportunities to work in incredible ways.*

Digging Deeper

This passage shows that the widow was committed to worshipping, fasting, and praying in the temple night and day. Her life was probably considered simple to some, but her wholehearted commitment to God is inspiring. Anna was privileged enough to get to see the fulfillment of all she had hoped and prayed for in the infant Jesus.

Chapter 2: The Freedom of Simplicity

Focus: *When you're facing a giant, it's easy to lose perspective. God invites us to turn to Him, keep our eyes on Him, and remain faithful to Him. This may seem like a simple response, but it's a powerful one.*

1. *Giants may include busy schedules, financial situations, health issues, stress, or relationship troubles. Gently remind the participants that instead of focusing on our giants, we should focus on the power of God in our lives. With God, anything is possible.*

2. *Answers will vary. As people respond, you may want to make notes for a prayer time at the end of the lesson.*

3. *Goliath donned a helmet of bronze, a coat of scale armor, bronze greaves (shin guards), a javelin, a spear, and a shield. Dressed as a shepherd rather than a warrior, David approached Goliath with the simple tools of a shepherd: a staff, five smooth stones, his bag, and a sling.*

4. *Answers will vary. We all have different emotional and practical responses to the giants we face. Some people may reach for prayer and faith in God to protect themselves. Others may prefer the support of Christian community, worship, or studying the*

Scriptures. Once you realize that God is bigger than any giant, it is easier to release your fears and trust in Him.

5. *"Am I a dog, that you come to me with sticks?" And the Philistine cursed David by his gods. And the Philistine said to David, "Come to me, and I will give your flesh to the birds of the air and the beasts of the field!" (1 Samuel 17:43–44).*

6. *Then David said to the Philistine, "You come to me with a sword, with a spear, and with a javelin. But I come to you in the name of the LORD of hosts, the God of the armies of Israel, whom you have defied. This day the LORD will deliver you into my hand, and I will strike you and take your head from you. And this day I will give the carcasses of the camp of the Philistines to the birds of the air and the wild beasts of the earth, that all the earth may know that there is a God in Israel. Then all this assembly shall know that the LORD does not save with sword and spear; for the battle is the LORD's, and He will give you into our hands" (1 Samuel 17:45–47).*

7. *Goliath thought that the source of his victory would be his fighting capabilities. On the other hand, David knew that the source of his victory was God.*

8. *Answers will vary, but we need to remember that God is the source of our victory, not ourselves. Suggest that the group rewrite David's speech on a note card and post it somewhere they can see it often. Then it can be a constant reminder to praise God in victory.*

Digging Deeper

Although we may try to, sometimes it becomes difficult to lift up all of our anxieties to God. Instead, we try to juggle them along with daily life. God will grant you peace if you give Him your worry and strife. "Whatever things are true, whatever things are noble, whatever things are just, whatever things are pure, whatever things are lovely, whatever things are of good report, if there is any virtue and if there is anything praiseworthy—meditate on these things" (Philippians 4:8).

Chapter 3: The Joy of Simplicity

Focus: *Knowing and obeying God and following His commands—no matter how simple they seem—will fill you with joy overflowing.*

1. *Answers will vary. Some people will prefer a nap, others to engage in the outdoors, and still others find joy in listening to music. After the participants share, point out that most of the things that renew us are incredibly simple things.*

2. *Answers will vary, but encourage participants to engage in the activities that help renew and refresh them.*

3. *Answers will vary. At times obeying God is challenging, but joy results.*

4. *We are told to love God with all our hearts, souls, and strength. The passage in Deuteronomy is asking us to love God with our whole entire being, and nothing less. Loving God can be done through obeying Him, praising Him, thanking Him, and worshipping Him. We can love God by talking to Him, being*

honest with Him, and so much more. Encourage participants to share creative expressions of loving God.

5. *Some ideas may include meditating on different Scriptures daily, having a family devotional, or posting Scripture around your house. It is interesting to note that Jews used to wear a box containing the **Shema** on their heads (called **phylacteries**) when they prayed. Many Orthodox Jews still wear these today.*

6. *By loving God, you will want to serve Him and follow His commandments. By loving others, Jesus does not just mean an abstract love, but rather an obligation to serve others and meet their needs.*

7. *Answers:*

Scripture Reference	Benefit of Following God's Commands
John 14:15–17	The Holy Spirit will be sent to you.
1 John 5:3–5	You will overcome the world.
Joshua 1:8	You will be prosperous and successful.
Proverbs 10:27	Your lives will be lengthened.
Deuteronomy 28:1–13	Blessings await you, and you will be set high above the nations on earth.

8. *Answers will vary. Sometimes it is hard to follow even the simplest commandments, but when we do, we will reap the benefits. By loving God, we can be changed and transformed by His power. Through loving others, we are able to pour out the love of God onto others, reflecting His character.*

Digging Deeper

A child becomes a metaphor of discipleship. Rather than making oneself great through acts, a child knows he is defenseless without the help of his parents. Children are dependent by nature. By child-like faith, we are able to humble ourselves in order to receive God's grace and mercy.

Chapter 4: Discovering What You Really Need

Focus: *Jesus promises to meet all of our needs, but not all of our wants.*

1. *This would be a huge change in spending habits for most participants, one that would force creativity and intentionality.*

2. *Answers will vary.*

3. *Answers will vary.*

4. *Answers will vary.*

5. *Many times, the objects we may find in our living spaces won't be necessary things, but instead just stuff we wanted. While this exercise is not supposed to deter spending of any kind, it is designed to open our eyes to real necessities.*

6. *"Give us this day our daily bread" (Matthew 6:11).*

7. *Both the manna in Exodus and the Lord's Prayer are reminders of our dependence on God.*

8. *By asking for our daily bread, we are allowing God to provide for us just as much or as little as He knows we need, and trusting Him for it.*

Digging Deeper

If we trust God as our Shepherd, He will provide for all our needs, and we will not be lacking. To lack nothing means to have no worries or anxiety about tomorrow, but rather to rest in God's assurance of love and peace. We would be less likely to be stressed if we fully trusted God to provide our daily bread.

Chapter 5: Celebrating God Moments

Focus: *God has a way of surprising us with Himself. Keep your eyes, ears, and hearts open to the God moments when He wants to reveal Himself to you.*

1. *Answers will vary. Highlight the idea that everyone has projects and activities that they need to get done. For many of us, the list may seem never ending, but that's okay. We can still find joy and delight in the midst of much to do.*

2. *Gently encourage participants to think of a few people they've meant to call, e-mail, or grab a bite to eat with, and make the time to get together. Sometimes reconnecting with others is like a breath of fresh air—it gives life to our own souls as well as others.*

3. *Participants may experience God moments at all different times in daily life. Celebrate the different ways God gets our attention.*

4. *Sometimes God uses similar things in our lives to draw our hearts back to His own. For some people, music may be important to experiencing God and His presence. Others may be more likely to encounter God when they're out in nature or in a church service. Others may experience God in the midst of community and Christian fellowship. Encourage participants to notice any patterns in the way God gets their attention and draws their hearts back to His.*

5. *The women were taking spices to the tomb to prepare Jesus' body for death. They were shocked when they saw two men standing in front of them announcing that Jesus had been raised from the dead. The women were trying to mark something off their "to-do" list when it came to funeral arrangements, and the angels announced there wasn't going to be a funeral. Jesus was alive.*

6. *The men were busy traveling to Emmaus when Jesus appeared to them, though they didn't recognize Him. He explained many spiritual things to them. In fact, the Scripture says the distance they traveled to Emmaus was about seven miles. If they walked fifteen-minute miles, one can estimate that they spent nearly two hours together.*

7. *The disciples were talking among themselves about all that had happened. Jesus suddenly stood among them and instructed them to wait until they had been clothed in power. Then He ascended into heaven before them. This must have been a shocking scene for everyone.*

8. *Answers will vary, but we can be responsive to the moments when God wants to get our attention. We may need to slow down, change our pace, or even alter our plans.*

Digging Deeper

Abram was ninety-nine years old (v. 1). Right off the bat, God changed Abram's name to Abraham. He told Abraham many prophetic things: that he would be the father of many nations (v. 4), that God would establish a covenant with Abraham (v. 7), and that He would give Abraham land (v. 8). From the moment God called Abram, his life was forever changed. Answers will vary, but God created us and knows which ways work best to get our attention. The life of Abraham is encouraging for people because God chose to use him and have a God moment with him despite his age or profession.

Chapter 6: Taking Time to Reflect

Focus: *When we choose to reflect on life, we get a chance to gain a healthy perspective, sort through priorities, and make the most of life. We move from passing the time in* chronos *moments to truly living a* kairos *life.*

1. *Answers will vary.* **Chronos** *activities may include things like punching a clock for work, spending thirty minutes on a treadmill, or commuting an hour to work. Those same activities can become* **kairos** *activities when we look for opportunities to use the gifts God has given us for His glory while we're at work, when our time on the treadmill fills us with energy and strength, and when our drive to work is spent thanking God for all the good things we've been given.*

2. *Answers will vary, but many people feel the pressure of the clock. We feel the deadlines and pressures and busyness and can forget the delight of the projects and activities we're involved in.*

3. *Answers will vary, but sometimes the only difference between a* **chronos** *and a* **kairos** *moment is a difference in perspective.*

4. *Though God did a lot of work during the first six days of creation, He didn't take the seventh day off because He was tired. God rested as an example for all of us that we, too, need rest. We need to be intentional about taking time to unplug and avoid work.*

5. *Answers will vary, but it's obvious that honoring the Sabbath was very important to God. It's interesting to note that God took more time to explain the purpose and specifics of this commandment than any of the others. It also highlights the idea that God began demonstrating the need for rest even in the creation story of Genesis 2:2–3.*

6. *The Pharisees were concerned that Jesus and His disciples were not keeping the Sabbath, which was an important religious practice, as examined in Exodus 20. The Pharisees may have been justified in their own minds regarding their response, but they missed out on the real heart of the commandment. The Sabbath was never meant to prevent people from helping others, loving, or serving.*

7. *Answers will vary, but Jesus responded to those who were concerned with the Law with a Law-based response. He pointed out that there are times in Scripture where it is clearly demonstrated that feeding and helping others on the Sabbath is good to do. Jesus didn't just answer the Pharisees with words. He also responded in action. Matthew 12:9 says that Jesus went into the Pharisees' synagogue.*

Think about that. He went right into their religious institution to show them what He was about. On the spot, He healed a man on the Sabbath, demonstrating that the law of love is greater than the law of religious rules.

8. *Answers will vary, but some people may take off different days of the week based on their work schedule. Others may find that getting away to a retreat center or even a quiet room in the house can make a huge difference when it comes to finding renewal and refreshment. Making time to rest or reflect takes time and preparation. We may complete certain activities—like laundry—before we can get away, but a little preparation can go a long way to truly being able to unplug and reflect.*

Digging Deeper

Answers will vary, but taking a Sabbath is a great way to feel refreshed and delighted in the Lord. For some, this allows them to catch up on much-needed rest. For others, it permits them to spend time in fellowship with others. Some take the Sabbath to refocus their lives on God. Once you are reenergized and ready for another week, you are able to get away from the everyday routine and discover more joy. Busy schedules and the *chronos* moments of life can take over and remove any Sabbath from our planning. However, once we choose to make taking a Sabbath a priority, we are able to sit back and rejuvenate our lives.

Chapter 7: Say Farewell to Insecurity

Focus: *Simplifying our lives means dealing with the things—both tangible and intangible—that weigh us down, including insecurities.*

1. *Insecurity has a way of making our relationships muddier than they need to be. Insecurities can cause us to make unhealthy choices in all areas of our lives. We may choose to buy things to make ourselves feel better, but get in debt. We may choose to avoid someone because we feel inferior, but miss out on an amazing relationship. We may pass on an opportunity at work or church or in our community because insecurity gets the best of us—and then find ourselves regretting it later on.*

2. *Answers will vary but all of us have different situations—whether it's meeting new people, traveling to new places, or trying new things—that make us feel unsure about ourselves.*

3. *Answers will vary. Some people try to ignore insecurities while others allow them to hold them back. Encourage participants to note that everyone has insecurities, and one of the first ways to move beyond an insecurity is to notice that you have one and recognize how you respond.*

4. *Answers will vary, but knowing that God knows us so well can be an incredible source of encouragement.*

5. *Answers will vary, but knowing that God made a masterpiece when He made us is essential. It will change the way we look at ourselves, others, and our own faith journey. Insecurities disappear when we know God has made us for His purposes.*

6. *Answers will vary, but the psalmist reminds us that God is ultimately the source of our protection and strength. He is the first one we should turn to.*

7. *Answers:*

Scripture Reference	Scripture
Psalm 56:3–4	"Whenever I am afraid, I will trust in You. In God (I will praise His word), in God I have put my trust; I will not fear. What can flesh do to me?"
Isaiah 41:10	"Fear not, for I am with you; Be not dismayed, for I am your God. I will strengthen you, Yes, I will help you, I will uphold you with My righteous right hand."
John 14:1	"Let not your heart be troubled; you believe in God, believe also in Me."
John 16:33	"These things I have spoken to you, that in Me you may have peace. In the world you will have tribulation; but be of good cheer, I have overcome the world."

8. *Answers will vary. These passages are reminders that we don't need to fear or feel insecure, because God is on our side.*

Digging Deeper

Imitating Christ means humbling yourself to the stature of a servant (v. 7). To serve someone means to put his or her needs above your own. When we do that, we no longer have our problems and insecurities in mind, but rather think only of the person we are serving.

Chapter 8: Letting Go of Unhealthy Patterns

Focus: *Sometimes we lose simplicity when unhealthy patterns appear in our lives. God wants us to experience freedom and wholeness in every area of our lives.*

1. *Answers will vary, but most of us have times when we struggle to maintain spiritual disciplines because of the busyness of life.*

2. *While some healthy patterns may be easy—for example, if you love eating salad every night, then eating vegetables as part of dinner may come easily for you—often healthy patterns take some level of commitment and discipline. Often there's a reward for making healthy choices.*

3. *While we can choose to actively pursue unhealthy patterns, most of us find that they slip into our lives when we're not paying attention, tired, or busy. We may have every intention to eat healthy home-cooked meals, but find ourselves living on fast food because of all the day's demands.*

4. *Jesus told Zacchaeus to come down from the tree and invited Himself to Zacchaeus's house. The people watching were bothered that Jesus would spend time with a cheat like Zacchaeus.*

5. *The tax collector responded to Jesus immediately. He welcomed Jesus into his home, offered to give half of his possessions to the poor, and paid back anyone he'd cheated four times the amount.*

6. *Jesus told the rich young ruler that he needed to follow the commandments. When the ruler didn't feel like that was enough, Jesus asked him to sell everything and follow Him.*

7. *The rich ruler became sad and didn't want to give up his wealth to follow Jesus, whereas Zacchaeus volunteered to give to the poor and make restitution to everyone he had cheated.*

8. *Answers will vary. We need to respond quickly to the nudging of God in our lives. If we feel that we need to make a change, we should do so quickly and generously.*

Digging Deeper

The woman caught in adultery probably felt many emotions, including guilt, fear, shame, anger, disappointment, loss, agony, despair, confusion, hope, bewilderment, strength, and joy. Jesus told her to go and leave her life of sin. The change was probably hard on the woman, but she knew she had to make it. Her unhealthy patterns had almost cost her life. When it comes to breaking free from unhealthy patterns, we need God. He is the source of our strength, hope, and freedom.

Chapter 9: So Long, Guilt

Focus: *Guilt is one of the heaviest pieces of baggage we can try to carry around. God doesn't want us to feel guilty but to experience the freedom and forgiveness He offers.*

1. *Answers will vary, but most of us have felt guilty for something we've done that was unkind or hurtful or absentminded. As children of God, we don't have to carry around the guilt. We can ask God to forgive us, and if possible, we can ask the other person to forgive us too. Because of our upbringings and experiences, most people respond to guilt differently.*

2. *Answers will vary.*

3. Answers will vary.

4. The psalmist described the guilt he felt for his wrongdoing as a heavy burden. Guilt often feels heavy. It can pierce our hearts and make us feel weak and vulnerable.

5. David responded to the sin in his life by confessing his sin to God, and God was faithful to forgive him.

6. Answers:

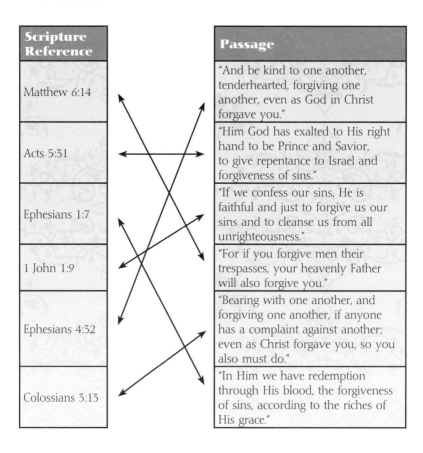

Scripture Reference	Passage
Matthew 6:14	"And be kind to one another, tenderhearted, forgiving one another, even as God in Christ forgave you."
Acts 5:31	"Him God has exalted to His right hand to be Prince and Savior, to give repentance to Israel and forgiveness of sins."
Ephesians 1:7	"If we confess our sins, He is faithful and just to forgive us our sins and to cleanse us from all unrighteousness."
1 John 1:9	"For if you forgive men their trespasses, your heavenly Father will also forgive you."
Ephesians 4:32	"Bearing with one another, and forgiving one another, if anyone has a complaint against another; even as Christ forgave you, so you also must do."
Colossians 3:13	"In Him we have redemption through His blood, the forgiveness of sins, according to the riches of His grace."

7. *It's comforting to know that God forgives us and we don't have to live under the burden of guilt.*

8. *Answers will vary. Participants may need to apologize to someone, spend time talking to God about an issue, or learn to forgive themselves for something they've done.*

Digging Deeper

Jesus was greeted by John the Baptist as the "Lamb of God who takes away the sin of the world." This is significant because forgiveness is in the heart of God and the nature of Jesus Christ. Jesus died that we might be forgiven for all our sin. Knowing this gives us the courage and strength to pursue a relationship with Jesus no matter what we've done in the past. Our future is secure in Jesus.

Chapter 10: Budding with Generosity

Focus: *Gifts don't have to be complex to be generous expressions of our love of God and others. Sometimes the simplest gift is the most meaningful.*

1. *Elijah was anything but shy when it came to his requests from the widow. He asked for food and water, and the woman responded with hospitality and honesty. While she didn't initially offer Elijah bread, she did make his bread first as a sign of faith that the prophet's words would come true.*

2. *Answers will vary, but often God can do amazing things through our gifts, no matter how small or insignificant they may be.*

3. *Answers will vary. Some people find it easy to give presents, money, kind words, or time, while others may find those same things more difficult.*

4. *Answers will vary, but Jesus noted that the widow who gave the smallest amount actually gave more than all the other contributors. Rather than giving out of her excess, she gave everything.*

5. *Answers will vary. Encourage participants to share specific examples of gifts that have been the most meaningful to them. The Scripture says that God loves a cheerful giver (2 Corinthians 9:7) and He loves it when we give in response to Him, and what He's done in our lives.*

6. *Answers:*

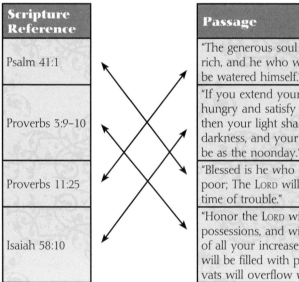

Scripture Reference	Passage
Psalm 41:1	"The generous soul will be made rich, and he who waters will also be watered himself."
Proverbs 3:9–10	"If you extend your soul to the hungry and satisfy the afflicted soul, then your light shall dawn in the darkness, and your darkness shall be as the noonday."
Proverbs 11:25	"Blessed is he who considers the poor; The LORD will deliver him in time of trouble."
Isaiah 58:10	"Honor the LORD with your possessions, and with the firstfruits of all your increase; so your barns will be filled with plenty, and your vats will overflow with new wine."

7. *Answers will vary.*

8. *Answers will vary.*

Digging Deeper

People were giving of their talents, their time, and their physical resources. God used the gifts of many people to build the tabernacle—a place where God would dwell. People gave as they could. They gave faithfully and regularly, and there was more than enough.

Chapter 11: Celebrating with Peace

Focus: *God provides peace—a kind of peace that floods our hearts and lives with contentment despite what may be going on around us.*

1. *Answers will vary. Encourage participants to share honestly about where they are in their lives.*

2. *Answers will vary, but often we think of God's peace in the absence of conflict or challenges. It's worth noting that He is in both—God's peace is accessible to us all the time. We may be aware of our need for His peace in one situation more than the other, but the actual need for God and His peace is the same regardless.*

3. *Encourage participants to share from their lives and experiences.*

4. *Paul instructed Timothy to resist temptations, including greed, and pursue righteousness, godliness, faith, love, endurance, and gentleness. He challenged Timothy to hold on to his faith and pursue holiness. The journey would probably not be easy for Timothy, and Paul wanted to encourage his young friend to remain strong.*

5. *On several occasions in the Scriptures, including Ephesians 6:10–18, the journey of faith is described using a battle metaphor. Growing in our faith can feel like a fight at times, as we make choices that go against our natural desires, but the rewards for faithfulness are immeasurable.*

6. *Jesus promised His disciples that the Counselor, the Holy Spirit, was going to come and remind them of everything Jesus had taught them. In addition, Jesus was giving them peace—His peace.*

7. *Answers will vary, but Jesus wants His disciples to know that the peace He gives is truly a gift from God. It cannot be replicated. God alone can provide this kind of peace.*

8. *Answers will vary. The world views peace one way, but Jesus offers a different kind of peace. The world's peace may be superficial, but the peace offered by God is perfect and fulfilling.*

Digging Deeper

We are invited to live according to the Spirit and not according to our sinful nature. Sexual immorality, impurity, idolatry, witchcraft, hatred, and much more are not according to the spirit. Instead we are to live in response to the Spirit. When we do, we'll find the fruits—love, joy, peace, patience, kindness, goodness, faithfulness, gentleness, and self-control—sprouting up in our lives.

Chapter 12: Living with Graciousness

Focus: *The fruit of simplicity is that you have more margin to take time to be kind, respond to needs, and honor others above yourself. In the process, you'll find yourself growing in ways you never imagined.*

1. *Answers will vary, but God challenges us all in different ways. We may be growing in patience or love or compassion for others. The change in our hearts may be because of a particular person or situation or the result of an age or stage in life.*

2. *Often the most challenging ones are the ones that give us the biggest opportunity to grow.*

3. *Answers:*

   Psalm 86:15: Compassionate, gracious, slow to anger, and abounding in love and faithfulness.

   Psalm 103:8: Compassionate, gracious, slow to answer, abounding in love.

   Psalm 111:4: Gracious and compassionate.

4. *Knowing that God is compassionate and gracious reminds us that He is the source of compassion and grace. We can turn to Him for help and ask that His love flow through us. All of us have situations that challenge our ability to be gracious. Yet even when we don't feel compassion or love for someone at the moment, God still does.*

5. *As children of God, we are to be transformed by the renewing of our minds, walk in humility, and recognize that we all have different gifts. We need to put those gifts to use no matter which gifts we've been given. Some will serve, some will teach, some will give, some will lead, some will govern, and some will show mercy— among other gifts.*

6. *Answers will vary. As a leader, consider finding a spiritual gifts quiz or survey and have your group participate. It is helpful as an individual and in a group setting to understand the various gifts that God has given them.*

7. *Answers will vary. It's amazing to think how simple the message of Jesus really is. We are to love others and love God above all else. When we do those things, all the things that Paul described in Romans 12 are simple to follow. Sometimes we are the ones who make faith complex because we overthink it or try too hard instead of relying on Jesus as our source.*

8. *Answers will vary.*

Digging Deeper

By obeying what Jesus asks in Matthew 6:1–4, we don't feel that we need to impress or prove ourselves to anyone. The only thing that matters is that we do it out of a giving, gracious heart. Answers will vary.

Notes

Chapter 1

1. Mark Buchanan, *The Rest of God* (Nashville: Thomas Nelson, 2006), 42–43.

Chapter 5

1. William Haefeli, "You're on our 'to do' list" (cartoon), *The New Yorker*, August 20, 2007, 58.

Chapter 7

1. http://www.powertochange.ie/changed/jonathan_edwards.html (story no longer available on site).

Chapter 8

1. R. Kent Hughes, *Disciplines of a Godly Man* (Wheaton, IL: Crossway, 1991), 105.

Chapter 11

1. Adapted from Berit Kjos, A *Wardrobe from the King* (Wheaton, IL: Victor, 1988), 45–46.

Chapter 12

1. Glen Van Ekeren, *Speaker's Sourcebook II* (New York: Prentice Hall, 2002), 180.

About the Author

A popular speaker at churches and leading conferences such as Catalyst and Thrive, Margaret Feinberg was recently named one of the '30 Emerging Voices' who will help lead the church in the next decade by *Charisma* magazine and one of the '40 Under 40' who will shape Christian publishing by Christian Retailing, she has written more than two dozen books and Bible studies including the critically-acclaimed *The Organic God, The Sacred Echo, Scouting the Divine* (Zondervan) and their corresponding DVD Bible studies. She is known for her relational teaching style and inviting people to discover the relevance of God and His Word in a modern world.

Margaret and her books have been covered by national media including: *CNN, the Associated Press, Los Angeles Times, Dallas Morning News, Washington Post, Chicago Tribune, Newsday, Houston Chronicle, Beliefnet.com, Salon.com, USATODAY.com, MSNBC.com, RealClearPolitics.com, Forbes.com,* and many others.

About the Author

Margaret currently lives in Morrison, Colorado, with her 6'8"
husband, Leif. When she's not writing or traveling, she enjoys anything outdoors, lots of laughter, and their superpup, Hershey. But
she says some of her best moments are spent communicating with
her readers. So go ahead, drop her a note:

> Margaret Feinberg
> PO Box 441
> Morrison, CO 80465
> www.margaretfeinberg.com
> info@margaretfeinberg.com
> Become a fan on Facebook
> Follow on twitter: @mafeinberg.

Additional Resources

What Shall We Study Next?

Women of Faith® has numerous study guides available
that will draw you closer to God.

Visit www.womenoffaith.com or www.thomasnelson.com
for more information.

Discovering God in Your Creativity
You Are Made in the Image of a Creative God

*In the beginning God created the
heavens and the earth.*

GENESIS 1:1

The initial splash of creativity is displayed in the first words of the Bible: "In the beginning God created. . . ." With those words, God took the plunge into designing the cosmos and the earth. As the first chapters of Genesis reveal, God did not hold back! He created a spectrum of colors, tastes, smells, and sounds.

Today we still enjoy the bounty of all God has made and formed. If you're an early riser, then you know the sunrise is a work of art in and of itself. Some mornings it looks as if God has finger-painted the sky. For those who prefer to sleep in, God makes sure you don't miss His handiwork either, as sunsets reveal colors unimaginable. With vibrant hues of fuchsias, olives, and cerulean blues, God's color spectrum far exceeds that of a Crayola 164-Pack.

This study is designed to douse you in the creativity of God as if it were a cool spring on a hot summer day. My hope is that you'll decide to make time to pull off your shoes and experience the delight that comes with trying something new and unexpected. You may just find yourself refreshed and rejuvenated in ways you never imagined!

We live in a world where we're constantly pressed with demands on every side—from our work, our home, and our families. While many of those requirements are good, if they stack up too high, they can squeeze the life and the creativity out of us. We can become too busy and even too exhausted to engage in our creative pursuits. But that was never what God intended. God wants us to think creatively and express our love for Him and others creatively.

My hope and prayer is that through this study you will once again become awestruck by the Creator of the universe and all He has done and is continuing to do through your life. May you unlock your inner creativity in such a way that it makes a tangible difference, not only in your life, but also in the lives of those around you.

Blessings,

Margaret Feinberg

Experiencing Peace
With God, You Can Live Beyond Fear

The Lord gives strength to his people; the
Lord blesses his people with peace.

PSALM 29:11, NIV

Have you ever had something totally rock your world? You're going through life with sunny skies and smooth sailing when, seemingly out of nowhere, you're hit with a storm that takes your breath away. Just minutes before you were quiet, calm, and collected, but now you wonder, *What happened? Am I going to lose everything? What's going to save me this time?*

The truth is, becoming a follower of Jesus doesn't make all the storms of life head in the opposite direction. Sometimes they'll still blow our way. But when those storms come, we find ourselves clinging to an anchor, tucked away inside a cove, and safely harbored in the arms of God. God never intended us to live in fear. He designed us to walk in faith. Even as we're making that journey, we'll still encounter challenges, trials, and difficult times. How do we face them? By embracing the peace of God.

When the Bible talks about peace, it usually refers to one of two types of peace: peace *with* God and the peace *of* God. Peace with God means through grace and the wondrous work Jesus did on the cross we can experience peace with God. But that's not all! We also get to enjoy the peace of God. Throughout the Scriptures we are reminded that we don't need to be anxious for a single thing. We can choose to trust God, pray, be thankful, and enjoy the contentment that comes with knowing God has everything under control. That doesn't mean that the peace of God is always easy to recognize according to outward circumstances. In fact, sometimes when things look their roughest and toughest on the outside, peace can reign on the inside. That's good news because it means the peace of God is not dependent on outward activity or happenstance.

By placing our trust in the Prince of Peace, we receive a peace that surpasses our wildest imaginations. My hope is that as you go through this study, you will fully embrace the peace that God gives you as His child.

Blessings,

Margaret Feinberg

Get Fresh . . .

Enthusiasm, Inspiration, Strength
at a **Women of Faith** weekend event!

At Women of Faith, thousands of women come together for two days to laugh, cry, worship, share, and draw strength from each other and from God. Messages, music, and more combine for a one-of-a-kind event designed by women for women.

"I'm always energized for months after attending these events!" –Angie G.

Join us at an event near you!

See details and sign up at **womenoffaith.com** or call 888-49-FAITH (888-493-2484).

*"God's presence was felt the very first moment we walked
in the door and never left!"* –Kellye H.

Don't Wait! Seats are Going Fast.

Bring your friends, bring your family, or just bring yourself . . . but whatever you do, don't miss this opportunity. Register today!